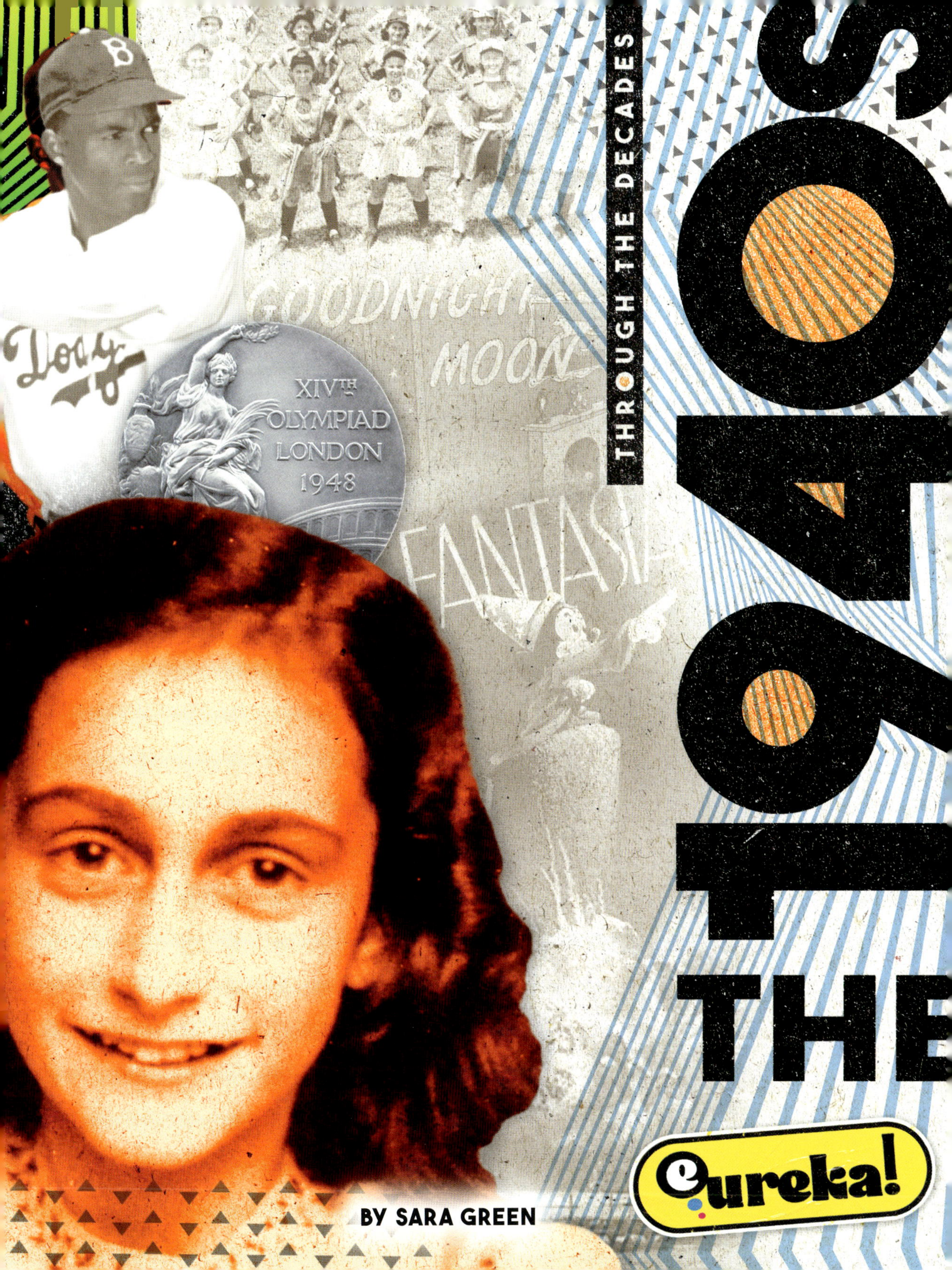
THE 1940s
THROUGH THE DECADES
GOODNIGHT MOON
FANTASIA
XIVTH OLYMPIAD LONDON 1948
BY SARA GREEN
eureka!

eureka!

Eureka! books turn real stories into unforgettable experiences. This nonfiction imprint sparks curiosity, encourages critical thinking, and engages middle-grade readers. *Eureka!* books empower young minds to explore the stories of the real world, one fascinating fact at a time. Unravel the power of knowledge and lifelong learning with *Eureka!*

This edition first published in 2026 by Bellwether Media, Inc.

Library of Congress Cataloging-in-Publication Data

LC record for The 1940s available at: https://lccn.loc.gov/2025021823

Editor: Rebecca Sabelko Series Designer: Andrea Schneider Book Designer: Laura Sowers

Printed in the United States of America, North Mankato, MN.

TABLE OF CONTENTS

WELCOME TO THE 1940s!

It is the summer of 1942. War is raging in Europe and across the Pacific. President Roosevelt has asked all Americans to support the troops however they can. One girl organizes a neighborhood scrap drive to collect paper, rubber, and tin foil. These items will be recycled into military supplies.

When the girl returns home, she puts a penny she found into a special savings jar in the kitchen. The family will use the money to buy war stamps that help the government fund the war. Next, she heads into her family's **Victory garden**. It is her turn to pull weeds. Despite the heat, the girl does not complain. She is happy to help her family grow their own food.

Later that afternoon, she and her family go to the theater to see an animated film called *Bambi*. They get there in time to see a cartoon before the movie starts. It features Mickey Mouse! A newsreel also plays. It covers what is happening overseas. An afternoon at the movies is the perfect reward for the girl's hard work!

WAR STAMP

MICKEY MOUSE

COLLECTING SCRAPS FOR A SCRAP DRIVE

VICTORY GARDEN

WHAT HAPPENED IN THE 1940s?

The 1940s were defined by World War II. In 1939, Nazi Germany, led by Adolf Hitler, invaded Poland. This triggered the start of the war in Europe. Most Americans favored **isolationism**. They felt the United States should not get involved in the war. This sentiment changed in 1941 when Japan attacked Pearl Harbor in Hawaii. The U.S. entered the war, sending troops to Europe and across the Pacific Ocean.

By 1943, the Nazis had overestimated their strength and suffered great defeats in Europe. Germany surrendered on May 7, 1945. The war in the Pacific was about to end, too. In August 1945, the U.S. dropped two **atomic bombs** on Japan. Japan surrendered on September 2, 1945.

By the end of the war, the U.S. and the **Soviet Union** had transformed into global superpowers. Many countries around the world benefited from a postwar economic boom, fueled in part by an increase in industry and **consumerism**. Meanwhile, tensions between the U.S. and the Soviet Union led to the start of the **Cold War**. This era of mutual distrust would last for decades.

ATTACK ON PEARL HARBOR

CHEESE PLEASE!

Hard cheese was easy to ship overseas to troops. At home, people ate cottage cheese instead. Kraft Macaroni and Cheese, called Kraft Dinner, was also hugely popular during the war years. It was cheap, easy to prepare, and could satisfy people's craving for cheese!

HOW MUCH?

1 GALLON GAS

$0.18 (1940)
$0.27 (1949)

THE NEW YORK TIMES
(late city edition)

$0.03 (1940) | $0.03 (1949)

1 GALLON MILK

$0.52 (1940)
$0.84 (1949)

MOVIE TICKET

$0.25 (1940)
$0.46 (1949)

CANDY BAR

$0.05 (1940)
$0.05 (1949)

BOTTLE OF COKE

$0.05 (1940)
$0.05 (1949)

LOAF OF BREAD

$0.10 (1940)
$0.14 (1949)

HISTORY

UNITED STATES HISTORY

Support for the troops was the U.S.'s main focus during World War II. Millions of men and more than 300,000 women served overseas in the armed forces. The war's demand for resources forced people to **ration** food, clothing, gasoline, and other items. Everyone, including children, received a book of stamps called a ration book that they used to buy rationed goods.

In 1940, nearly 8 million Americans were unemployed due to the **Great Depression**. The war effort created millions of new jobs, pulling the U.S. out of the Depression. Millions of women and minorities entered the workforce to fill jobs traditionally held by the men sent overseas.

The post-war years were marked by recovery and growth. Factories used to manufacture war-related products were retooled for other industries. Demand for single-family home ownership rose, leading to the growth of suburbs across the country.

RATION BOOK

WOMEN WORKING DURING WORLD WAR II

SUBURB

JAPANESE INTERNMENT

Anti-Japanese fears grew in the U.S. following the attack on Pearl Harbor. In response, the U.S. government forced more than 120,000 innocent Japanese Americans to move into internment camps. They lost their freedoms and their properties, and they were denied their constitutional rights. The last internment camp closed in 1946.

G.I. BILL

The G.I. Bill, signed into law by President Roosevelt on June 22, 1944, was created to help veterans readjust to civilian life after World War II. It provided benefits such as funds for education, home loans, and job training. These benefits helped the economy grow after World War II. Veterans still use the G.I. Bill today!

AN OFFICIAL APOLOGY

In 1988, Congress passed the Civil Liberties Act. The law acknowledged the injustices done to Japanese Americans and provided for a payment of $20,000 to each survivor of the internment camps.

PEACETIME DRAFT

The first peacetime draft was the Selective Training and Service Act of 1940 signed by President Roosevelt on September 16, 1940. The act required men between the ages of 21 and 45 to register for possible military service. The act expired at the end of World War II but was later reintroduced to maintain military strength during the Cold War.

choosing men for the draft

UNITED STATES POLITICS

In 1940, President Franklin Delano Roosevelt won a third term in office. He faced a country of citizens that mostly wanted to avoid the war. But he felt the U.S. needed to help its allies. He found a compromise. In 1941, Congress passed the Lend-Lease Act, which allowed the U.S. to provide aid to allies through supplies and equipment.

President Franklin Delano Roosevelt

ELECTION SHOWDOWN:
1940 PRESIDENTIAL ELECTION

ROOSEVELT (DEMOCRATIC)

WILLKIE (REPUBLICAN)

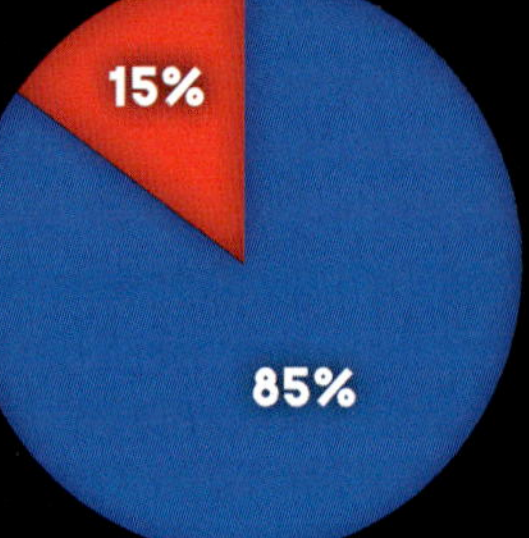

ELECTORAL VOTES

On December 7, 1941, Japan attacked Pearl Harbor. Within days, the U.S. was forced to declare war on Japan, Germany, and Italy, otherwise known as the Axis powers. President Roosevelt was elected to a fourth term in 1944. However, he died just months into his term. Vice President Harry S. Truman **succeeded** Roosevelt. His decision to drop atomic bombs on Japan ended the war but left hundreds of thousands of Japanese civilians dead or wounded. Effects of the bombs are still felt in Japan today.

In 1947, President Truman developed the Truman Doctrine to contain the spread of **communism**. It declared that the U.S. would provide military and financial aid to any country under the threat of communism. The Truman Doctrine would lead to U.S. intervention in world conflicts for decades to come.

NAGASAKI, JAPAN, ATOMIC BOMBING

PRESIDENT TRUMAN SIGNING THE TRUMAN DOCTRINE

THE MARSHALL PLAN

In 1948, the U.S. enacted the Marshall Plan to aid the economic recovery of war-torn Western Europe. It aimed to prevent the spread of communism and promote stability in the region.

U.S. FARMERS CARRYING OUT THE MARSHALL PLAN

SPOTLIGHT ON:

ATTACK ON PEARL HARBOR

Pearl Harbor is a U.S. naval base on the Hawaiian island of Oahu. On December 7, 1941, Japanese fighter planes staged an attack on Pearl Harbor just before 8 a.m. The air strike took the U.S. by surprise, even though Japan had been developing their plan for months. Japan wanted to take over several countries in Southeast Asia to gain power and resources in the region. They worried that the U.S. would send aid to these countries from Pearl Harbor, the closest military base to that region. In less than 90 minutes, around 20 U.S. naval vessels were damaged or sunk. More than 180 aircraft were destroyed or damaged. More than 2,300 people were killed, and another 1,000 people were wounded. However, the Japanese fighter planes missed oil tanks, ammunition sites, and other important military facilities. No U.S. aircraft carriers were on site during the attack.

The day after the attack, the U.S. declared war on Japan. The U.S. rebuilt and put back into service all but three of the battleships sunk or damaged at Pearl Harbor.

MAKING HEADLINES

"War! Oahu Bombed by Japanese Planes"

–*Honolulu Star-Bulletin,* December 7, 1941

"JAPANESE ATTACK ON HONOLULU BY AIR AND SEA IS 'BEATEN OFF'"

–*THE MILWAUKEE JOURNAL,* DECEMBER 8, 1941

PEARL HARBOR NATIONAL MEMORIAL

PRESERVING HISTORY

The Pearl Harbor National Memorial in Honolulu, Hawaii, is built on the water above the wreckage of the USS *Arizona*, one of the eight battleships attacked on December 7, 1941. Visitors can see the remains of the sunken ship lying 40 feet (12 meters) below the surface.

Navy Cross

DORIS MILLER

ROLE:
U.S. Navy Sailor

KNOWN FOR:
A U.S. Navy Sailor who served on the USS *West Virginia* during the attack on Pearl Harbor. Miller carried wounded individuals to safety. He also took charge of a machine gun to defend the ship against Japanese aircraft despite his lack of gunnery training. Miller was awarded the Navy Cross for his heroic actions, becoming the first Black Sailor to receive this honor.

WORLD HISTORY

Most of the world's nations were involved in World War II. The conflict was divided into two opposing military alliances. The main Allies consisted of Great Britain, the U.S., and the Soviet Union. The Axis Powers were led by Germany, Italy, and Japan. The war grew to become the largest and deadliest military conflict in history. It would eventually claim the lives of an estimated 60 million people, including 40 million civilians. World leaders created the United Nations (UN) in the aftermath of World War II to promote peace, cooperation, and diplomacy among nations. The UN Charter was signed in San Francisco, California, in 1945, with 51 founding members, including the U.S.

The 1940s also began to see colonized nations, such as British India, push for independence. But the transition to independence was sometimes violent. The division of British India into India and Pakistan resulted in religious political **rhetoric** that led to widespread violence and the death of thousands.

Battle of Iwo Jima, World War II

Signing of the UN Charter

Destruction during the division of British India

THE CREATION OF ISRAEL

In 1947, the UN voted to split Palestine into a Jewish state and an Arab state. The plan was to create an independent Israel for displaced Jewish people. Arab leaders did not approve of losing parts of their homeland. The disagreement resulted in the Arab-Israeli War of 1948. The conflict ended in Israel taking more Palestinian land. Hundreds of thousands of Palestinian Arabs became refugees. Tensions between the groups would continue well into the next century.

refugee camp

ATOMIC BOMBINGS OF HIROSHIMA AND NAGASAKI

In August 1945, the U.S. dropped atomic bombs on the Japanese cities of Hiroshima and Nagasaki. The bombs leveled the cities. They killed an estimated 100,000 to 200,000 people, mostly civilians. Many others were wounded. Days later, Japan surrendered to the U.S., ending World War II.

PEOPLE'S REPUBLIC OF CHINA

In 1949, Chinese Communist leader Mao Zedong announced the creation of the People's Republic of China. This ended years of civil war between the ruling Chinese Nationalist Party led by Chiang Kai-shek and the Chinese Communist Party led by Mao Zedong. Chiang Kai-shek fled to the island of Taiwan where he continued to rule as the leader of the Republic of China, which he declared the rightful government of China.

Mao Zedong

SPOTLIGHT ON:

THE HOLOCAUST

The Holocaust was the government-planned **persecution** and murder of six million Jews by the Nazi regime, its allies, and other supporters. It took place from 1933 to 1945 and remains one of the most horrifying events in history.

Adolf Hitler blamed Jewish people for Germany's loss in World War I. When the Nazis came into power in 1933, they began to strip Jewish people of their rights and properties. The Nazis forced Jews to live in ghettos and destroyed them economically. By 1941, the Nazis devised a plan called the "Final Solution" to systematically murder all Jewish people in Europe. They also targeted other groups they hated, including Romani people, people with disabilities, and gay people, as part of a senseless scheme to create a genetically superior "master race." The Nazis began putting Jewish people into concentration camps. Millions of people were killed by poisonous gas, including children. Many others died of exhaustion or disease. Others became victims of cruel medical experiments.

The first concentration camp was liberated by Allied troops in 1944. From 1945 to 1946, 24 former Nazi leaders were tried as war criminals in Nuremberg, Germany. Those found guilty received prison or death sentences.

MAKING HEADLINES

"GERMANS MURDER 700,000 JEWS IN POLAND"

—*DAILY TELEGRAPH*, JUNE 25, 1942

"Nazis Wiping Out Jews in Cold Blood"

—*Los Angeles Times*, November 25, 1942

"U.S. Verifies Mass Murders in German Prison Camps"

–The Salt Lake Tribune, November 26, 1944

Holocaust Memorial in Berlin, Germany

NEVER FORGOTTEN

In 2005, the UN's General Assembly designated January 27 as International Holocaust Remembrance Day to honor and remember the millions of people murdered by the Nazis.

SOCIAL CHANGES

World War II led to significant social changes. As men left to fight overseas, large numbers of women began working in factories and shipyards. Their new role was spurred on by a fictitious character named Rosie the Riveter. More than 300,000 women also joined the armed forces in noncombat roles.

U.S. society was hugely impacted once soldiers returned after the war. Many working women returned to domestic life. Some did so voluntarily, but others were forced out of the workforce by men returning home. A major increase in global birth rates, a phenomenon known as the baby boom, created increased demand for housing, education, and consumer goods. Low-interest home loans from the G.I. Bill drove the rapid expansion of suburban communities in the U.S.

Rosie the Riveter

Not everyone benefited from the economic growth. The U.S. was plagued by widespread **discrimination** and **segregation**, particularly in the South. Black Americans faced barriers to good jobs and home ownership. Black veterans were excluded from benefits of the G.I. Bill. These imbalances contributed to the widening wealth and education gap between white and Black Americans.

President Truman signed two executive orders in 1948 in an attempt to combat **racism**. The orders worked to end discrimination based on race, color, religion, or national origin. They helped fuel the growing civil rights movement.

WOMEN WORKING IN A FACTORY

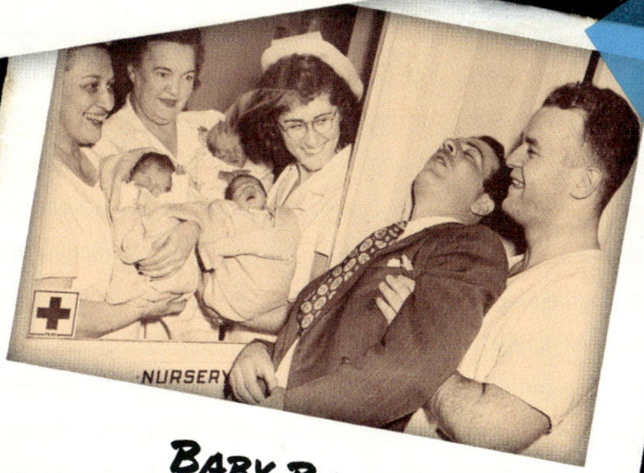

BABY BOOM

SEGREGATED BUS STATION

WOMEN IN SERVICE

More than 1,000 women flew military aircraft during the war. They did not fly in combat. Rather, they transported cargo, ferried planes to bases, and participated in simulation missions.

SCIENCE AND TECHNOLOGY

TECHNOLOGICAL ADVANCEMENTS

The 1940s saw important scientific and technological advancements. Many were sparked by the demands of World War II. Advances in **nuclear** technology led to the development of the atomic bomb that would help launch the Cold War. Radar technology also improved during the war. **Meteorologists** began to use this technology to better study and forecast the weather. One of the first general-purpose computers was announced in 1946 at the University of Pennsylvania. The Electronic Numerical Integrator and Computer (ENIAC) was programmed by a team of women. ENIAC took up 1,800 square feet (167 square meters).

Some war technologies later became commercial products. The device used in radar equipment became a crucial part of the microwave oven. Dr. Harry Coover invented Super Glue accidentally during his attempt to create clear plastic gun sights for the military.

MICROWAVE OVEN

INVENTOR:
Raytheon Company

YEAR INVENTED:
1945

EFFECT ON DAILY LIFE:
The first microwave ovens were about 6 feet (1.8 meters) tall and weighed more than 750 pounds (340 kilograms). Today, more than 9 in 10 American households have one. Microwave ovens reheat food, prepare frozen foods, pop popcorn, and even disinfect sponges!

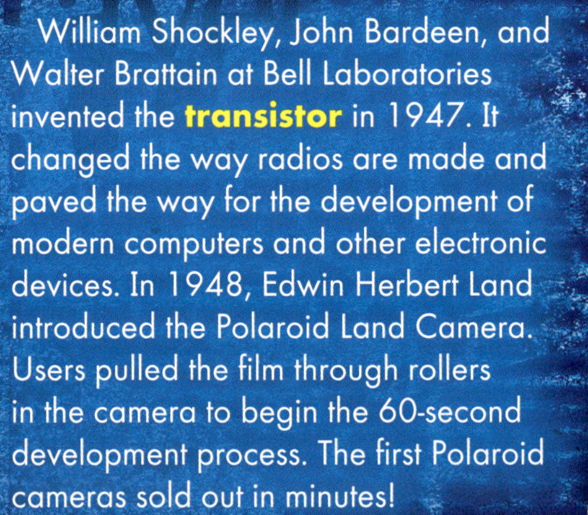

William Shockley, John Bardeen, and Walter Brattain at Bell Laboratories invented the **transistor** in 1947. It changed the way radios are made and paved the way for the development of modern computers and other electronic devices. In 1948, Edwin Herbert Land introduced the Polaroid Land Camera. Users pulled the film through rollers in the camera to begin the 60-second development process. The first Polaroid cameras sold out in minutes!

THE FIRST TRANSISTOR

ENIAC

DUCK OR DUCT?

In 1943, Vesta Stoudt suggested sealing ammunition cases with waterproof cloth tape. The Johnson & Johnson company soon developed a multi-purpose green cloth tape. Soldiers called it "duck" tape because it repelled water like duck feathers. After the war, people used a silver version to wrap air ducts. It became known as duct tape.

MEDICAL SCIENCE

World War II forced rapid advancements in medicine to aid wounded soldiers. These advancements would eventually become available to the civilian population and improve medical care for everyone. One of the most significant advancements was the widespread production of penicillin. This **antibiotic** treats potentially fatal bacterial infections. Another antibiotic called streptomycin was discovered in 1943. It became the first effective treatment for tuberculosis. In 1944, scientists created a drug called **synthetic** quinine to control malaria. This deadly disease is transmitted by mosquitoes and had been a significant threat to U.S. troops fighting in the South Pacific. The first flu vaccine was approved for military use in 1945. It became available to U.S. citizens a year later. The war also hurried the creation of cortisone. Cortisone revolutionized the treatment of inflammatory conditions such as asthma. Its ability to relieve pain led people to declare cortisone a miracle drug!

The war contributed to other advancements in health care. Surgeons developed new procedures in plastic surgery to repair soldiers' wounds. Many of them are still used today. An increased demand for blood **transfusions** led to the creation of blood banks and improvements in how blood is transported and stored.

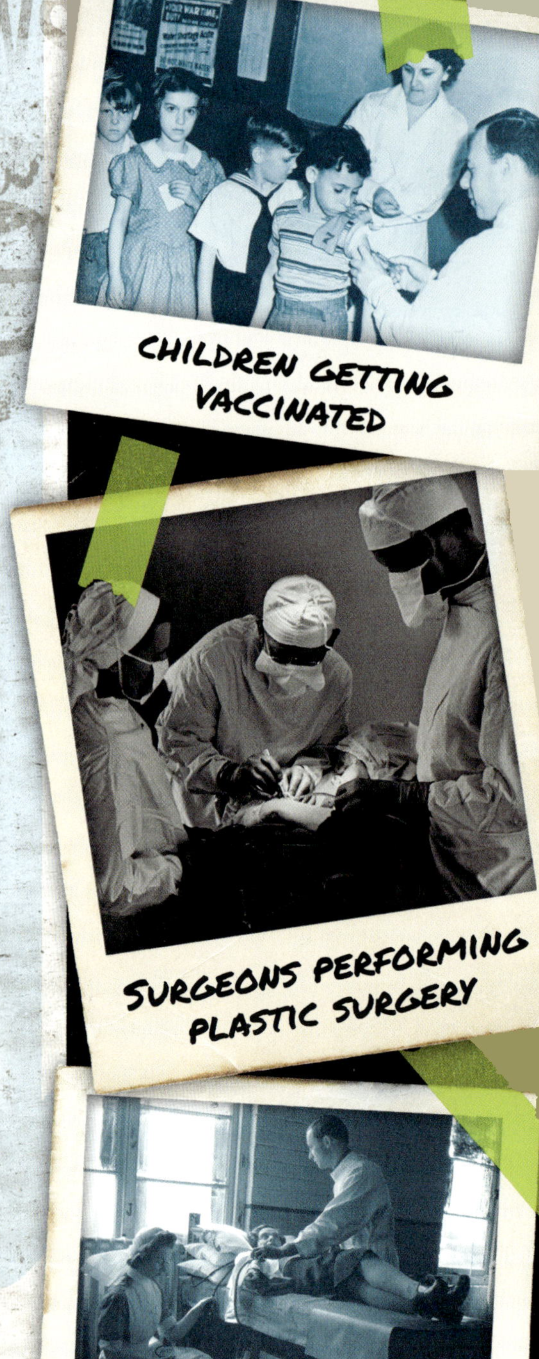
CHILDREN GETTING VACCINATED

SURGEONS PERFORMING PLASTIC SURGERY

DONATING BLOOD AT A BLOOD BANK

production of penicillin

DAILY LIFE

LIFE IN THE '40s

Daily life during the 1940s was deeply influenced by World War II. People had to ration many household goods, including food, gasoline, and clothing. Many families grew Victory gardens to supplement their food supply, leaving commercially grown food for the troops. People listened to radio broadcasts for news and entertainment and played board games with their families and friends. Although many families owned automobiles, fuel shortages led to the increased use of public transportation. People often relied on rail travel and bicycles for both short and long distances.

After the war ended, the G.I. Bill provided veterans with educational and housing opportunities. This, along with a postwar economic boom, led to the growth of the middle class and the suburbs. However, Black Americans continued to face discrimination. Oppressive rules called **Jim Crow laws** restricted the rights of Black people who lived throughout the South. The laws enforced racial segregation in most public places. They also did not allow interracial marriage.

WOMEN PLAYING A BOARD GAME

SEGREGATED WATER FOUNTAIN

ORIGINAL MCDONALD'S

In 1940, brothers Maurice and Richard McDonald opened the first McDonald's in San Bernardino, California. They began the Speedee Service System in 1948, introducing the idea of the fast-food restaurant.

1940s SLANG

Ducky Shincracker
A good dancer
Flip your Wig
Lose control of yourself
Cut a Rug
to dance
cool cat
An interesting or fashionable person
Off the Cob
silly
Hi-de-ho!
Hello!
Gobbledygook
Nonsense
Jeepers!
Exclamation of surprise

FASHION TRENDS

World War II impacted fashion trends of the early 1940s. Many supplies such as uniforms and parachutes caused fabric shortages. Simple styles became a necessity. Cuffs, ruffles, pleats, and other non-essential uses of fabric fell out of favor. Women wore wraparound skirts and dresses with shorter hemlines. Nylon stockings were scarce. Women applied makeup to their legs to mimic hosiery. Many even drew seam lines down the backs of their legs with eyeliner pencils!

WOMAN DRAWING A SEAM LINE ON LEG

Cab Calloway in a zoot suit

After the war ended, fabric was readily available again. An elegant style called the "New Look" became fashionable. Created by designer Christian Dior in 1947, this look featured long, flowy skirts, full sleeves, and tight waistlines. Women often wore their hair in Victory rolls or pin curls, two of the most popular hairstyles of the decade!

The war also affected men's fashions. Wartime Victory suits were muted in color and designed to use less fabric. They featured shorter jackets and straight-leg trousers. After the war, men embraced colorful shirts and bolder patterns. Men's suits featured wide shoulders, ties, and trousers. Zoot suits, especially popular with young men, featured oversized jackets with padded shoulders, baggy trousers, and wide-brimmed hats.

CHRISTIAN DIOR'S "NEW LOOK"

VICTORY SUITS

Victory rolls hairstyle

POOLSIDE FASHION

In 1946, French clothing designer Louis Réard introduced the modern bikini. It was named after the Bikini Atoll in the Pacific Ocean. This was the location of the first peacetime test of a nuclear bomb.

PRODUCTS AND TOYS

Toys and games brought great joy to children during the 1940s. During the war, families often made their own toys from scrap wood and other supplies. Toymakers used wood and paper to make paper dolls, puzzles, and other toys. War-themed toys, such as soldiers and toy guns, were also popular.

SLINKY

The Slinky is a coiled spring toy. It is known for being able to "walk" down stairs. The Slinky was accidentally invented by mechanical engineer Richard James in 1943. It became a sensation after James demonstrated it in 1945 at Gimbel's department store in Philadelphia.

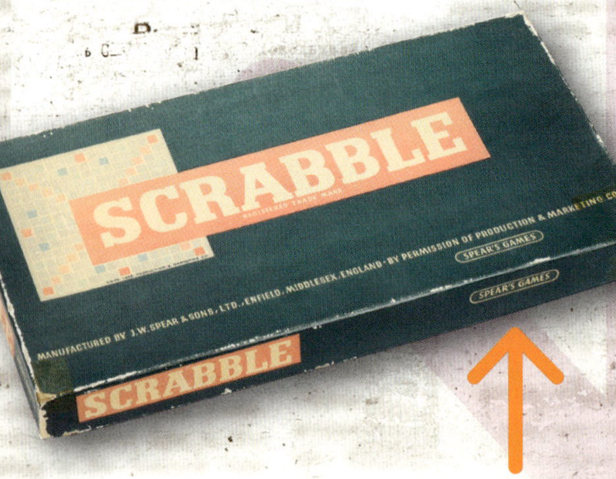

BOARD GAMES

Kids enjoyed playing board games such as Monopoly, Sorry!, and Scrabble. Candy Land, invented in 1948, was especially popular. It was named the American Toy Industry Association's most popular toy of the 1940s!

SUBBUTEO

Peter Adolph invented Subbuteo, a tabletop soccer game, in 1946. The original sets contained wire goals with paper nets, a ball, and cardboard figures weighted down with buttons and lead washers. The sets also included chalk and instructions on how to draw the playing field on a blanket.

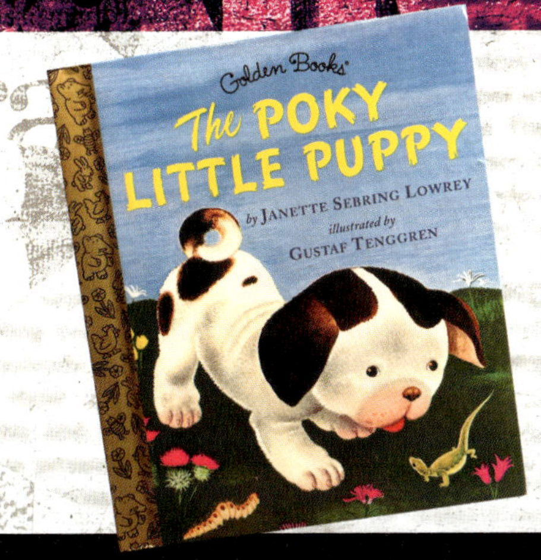

LITTLE GOLDEN BOOKS

Little Golden Books is a series of children's books published in the U.S. since 1942. Priced at 25 cents in the 1940s, Little Golden Books were affordable for most families. Children loved the delightful stories and cheerful illustrations. *The Poky Little Puppy*, written by Janette Sebring Lowrey and published in 1942, remains one of the top-selling children's books of all time!

MODEL TRAINS

Electric trains and model railroad sets were popular during the 1940s. American Flyer and Lionel were two of the most popular model train brands. They offered a variety of kits and accessories for hobbyists.

DOLLS

Dolls remained a favorite toy in the 1940s. The Ideal Toy Company was one of the first toy makers to make plastic dolls. Some of Ideal's most popular dolls during the 1940s were baby dolls, Hedwig dolls, and the Judy Garland doll.

BUBBLE SOLUTION

In 1940, a Chicago cleaning supplies company named Chemtoy began bottling and selling bubble solution. The bottles came with wands for making bubbles. Today, bubble solution is still one of the top-selling toys in the world!

ARTS AND ENTERTAINMENT

PUBLICATIONS

Wartime paper rationing did not stop people from reading. Demand for books remained high, especially on the battlefields. U.S. publishers gave away almost 123 million books to soldiers between 1943 and 1947. Many authors explored the war, racial conflict, and other serious issues of the time. Children were introduced to *Pat the Bunny* by Dorothy Kunhardt and *Goodnight Moon* by Margaret Wise Brown. These books are still beloved today!

People flipped through magazines such as *Life*, *TIME*, and *National Geographic* to get news and photos of world events and people's lives. *Seventeen*, the first modern magazine devoted to teens, debuted on newsstands in 1944. Original content focused on citizenship, careers, and fashion. Its popularity skyrocketed, with more than two million copies sold monthly by 1949.

READING REC

TITLE:
THE DIARY OF A YOUNG GIRL

AUTHOR:
Anne Frank

YEAR PUBLISHED:
1947

SUMMARY:
Anne Frank records her family's time in hiding as a Jewish teenager in Nazi-occupied Amsterdam during World War II.

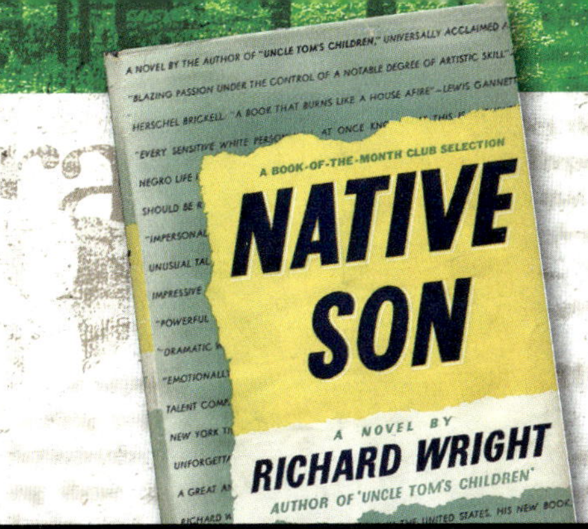

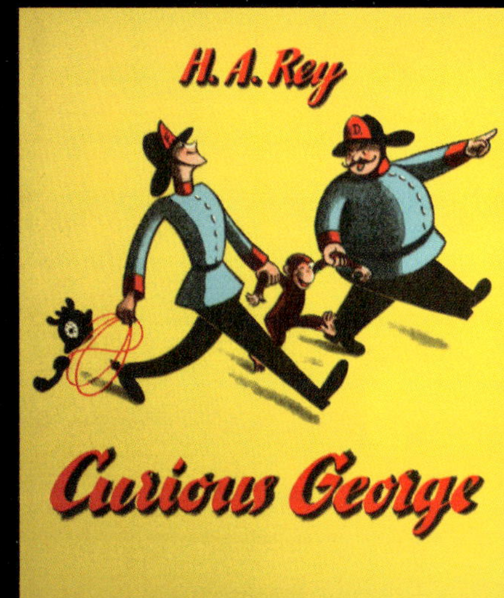

NATIVE SON

Native Son, published in 1940, tells the story of a young Black man angered by the oppression imposed by white society. The novel was a sensation and widely read by both Black and white readers. It made Richard Wright one of the country's first best-selling Black authors.

CURIOUS GEORGE

Curious George, written by H.A. Rey and Margaret Rey and published in 1941, was the first book in the Curious George series. It introduces readers to George, the mischievous monkey who lives with the Man with the Yellow Hat. The Curious George series has become a classic. Its tales of George's antics and adventures have delighted generations of children.

FOR WHOM THE BELL TOLLS

For Whom the Bell Tolls, written by Ernest Hemingway and published in 1940, is a novel set during the Spanish Civil War. It tells the story of an American man named Robert Jordan who volunteers to fight alongside Spanish fighters hiding in the mountains. The novel was an instant bestseller, with half a million copies sold within months of its publication.

George Orwell

ANIMAL FARM

Animal Farm, published in 1945, is a political allegory of the Russian Revolution and the rise of Stalinism. The novel is about a group of farm animals that overthrows their human owner and sets up their own egalitarian society only to have it fail. *Animal Farm* made George Orwell famous. Today, it is considered one of his best works.

MOVIES

Movies were a popular form of entertainment during the 1940s. The decade was part of Hollywood's Golden Age, known for its movie studio powerhouses and high-quality films. Glamorous movie stars such as Humphrey Bogart, Katherine Hepburn, and Ingrid Bergman became household names.

During the war years, many movies were set in World War II. Their anti-Nazi messages stirred up patriotism and lifted morale across the country. Dramatic films, including **film noir** and psychological thrillers, were popular after the war. Walt Disney Studios produced some of its greatest hits, including *Pinocchio*, *Dumbo*, and *Bambi*, during the decade.

The price of a movie ticket often included other entertainment. Before the movie started, audiences often watched a newsreel, a trailer, a short movie, and a cartoon. Bugs Bunny and other Looney Tunes characters were favorites!

Bugs Bunny

AT THE BOX OFFICE

TOP-GROSSING FILMS OF THE 1940s

- ***Bambi*** **(1942)**
- ***Pinocchio*** **(1940)**
- ***Fantasia*** **(1940)**
- ***Song of the South*** **(1946)**
- ***Mom and Dad*** **(1945)**
- ***Samson and Delilah*** **(1949)**
- ***The Best Years of Our Lives*** **(1946)**
- ***The Bells of St. Mary's*** **(1945)**
- ***This Is the Army*** **(1943)**
- ***Duel in the Sun*** **(1946)**

Pinocchio

FANTASIA

Walt Disney's animated film *Fantasia* was released in 1940. It consists of eight segments set to classical music. The movie features more than 500 animated characters, including Mickey Mouse in "The Sorcerer's Apprentice." It was one of the decade's top-grossing movies.

"The Sorcerer's Apprentice" from *Fantasia*

THE GREAT DICTATOR

The Great Dictator is a satire that mocks Adolf Hitler. It stars Charlie Chaplin, who also wrote and directed the movie. This film was Chaplin's first full "talkie," or movie with sound. The movie was banned in Germany but was a box office smash in the U.S.

FILM NOIR

Film noir is a type of suspenseful crime film that grew in popularity during the 1940s. The movies were filmed in black-and-white and often featured bleak settings and odd camera angles. *The Maltese Falcon* starring Humphrey Bogart is one of many film noir classics released in the 1940s.

CITIZEN KANE

Orson Welles starred in and directed *Citizen Kane,* a film about the life of a publishing giant. This groundbreaking film revolutionized cinematography and is often on lists of greatest movies ever made.

CASABLANCA

Casablanca is a romantic drama starring Humphrey Bogart and Ingrid Bergman. It is considered one of the greatest films of all time. *Casablanca* is set during World War II. It tells the story of an American who lives in Casablanca, Morocco, who must choose between love and politics.

TELEVISION AND RADIO

Radio was the main source of news and entertainment during much of the 1940s. People listened to music, radio shows, and wartime updates. Troops and civilians tuned in to the Armed Forces Radio Service, which first started broadcasting in 1943 from London, England.

Television was still in its beginnings at the start of the decade. In 1941, the CBS and NBC television networks began broadcasting 15 hours of programming a week. However, television sets were expensive and in limited supply. Most households did not own one. After the war ended, television production increased and sets became more affordable. By the decade's end, television was gaining widespread popularity. By 1950, more than five million households had a television set!

1940s radio

FIBBER McGEE AND MOLLY

Fibber McGee and Molly **was a radio comedy program starring Jim Jordan and Marian Driscoll Jordan. This real-life married couple played Fibber and his witty wife, Molly. The show also featured a cast of supporting characters who added laughs to each program.** ***Fibber McGee and Molly*** **was the most popular radio show on the air in 1941. Between 20 and 30 million listeners tuned in each week!**

CAPTAIN MIDNIGHT

Captain Midnight was a popular radio aviation adventure series that aired through the 1940s. Captain Midnight was a heroic pilot who flew around the world fighting evil enemies and rescuing people in distress. Listeners could use special series decoders to decipher encrypted messages broadcast during the show.

JACK ARMSTRONG, THE ALL-AMERICAN BOY

Jack Armstrong, the All-American Boy was a popular action-adventure radio show aimed at preteens and teens. Millions of kids would tune in after school to follow the adventures of Jack, a brave, athletic teenager, and his friends as they traveled the world. The show was sponsored by General Mills and Wheaties cereal.

Milton Berle

TEXACO STAR THEATER

A variety show called *Texaco Star Theater* was a popular television show. It started as a radio show in the 1930s before transitioning to television in 1948. The show starred comedian Milton Berle who became known as "Mr. Television" due to the show's great success. *Texaco Star Theater* helped boost the sales of television sets and popularize television.

MUSIC

Big band swing music was hugely popular during the 1940s. The upbeat, dance-style jazz music gave people relief from wartime worries.

Musical tastes started to shift later in the decade. Solo singers and small combos began to dominate the pop charts. A young singer named Frank Sinatra became a superstar. Rhythm and blues, a style of music that gave rise to rock and roll, emerged in the Black community and quickly gained popularity. The electric guitar, invented in the 1930s, transformed the blues sound during the 1940s by making it louder and more energetic!

HANK WILLIAMS

Hank Williams helped pioneer country music during the 1940s. Hit songs such as "Your Cheatin' Heart," "I'm So Lonesome I Could Cry," and "Hey, Good Lookin'" earned him millions of fans! Today, Hank Williams is still considered one of the genre's most influential artists.

1940s PLAYLIST

- ***In the Mood***
  Glenn Miller (1940)
- ***God Bless The Child***
  Billie Holiday (1941)
- ***White Christmas***
  Bing Crosby (1942)
- ***Paper Doll***
  The Mills Brothers (1943)
- ***Don't Fence Me In***
  Roy Rogers (1944)
- ***The Honeydripper***
  Joe Liggins & The Honeydrippers (1945)
- ***Ole Buttermilk Sky***
  Peggy Lee (1946)
- ***Scrapple from the Apple***
  Charlie Parker (1947)
- ***Buttons and Bows***
  Dinah Shore (1948)
- ***Lovesick Blues***
  Hank Williams (1949)

Dizzy Gillespie

BEBOP

Jazz music continued to evolve during the 1940s. Pianist Thelonious Monk, saxophonist Charlie Parker, and trumpeter Dizzy Gillespie introduced the world to a new type of jazz called bebop. It featured fast-paced improvisations and complex harmonies. Bebop was usually performed by small groups in front of audiences who wanted to listen to music instead of dance to it.

BIG BAND SWING

Big band swing was a style of jazz music that dominated the airwaves and dance halls during the early 1940s. Led by famous bandleaders such as Benny Goodman, Glenn Miller, Duke Ellington, and Count Basie, big bands played lively music that entertained millions during World War II.

The Duke Ellington Orchestra

CROONERS

Crooners were very popular in the 1940s. These singers were typically male and included artists Frank Sinatra, Bing Crosby, and Nat King Cole. They topped the charts with their smooth voices and romantic singing styles. Some of their hits, such as Bing Crosby's "White Christmas," are still favorites today!

THE ANDREWS SISTERS

The Andrews Sisters was one of the decade's most popular singing groups. The trio consisted of LaVerne, Maxene, and Patty Andrews. They often entertained troops during the war, earning them the nickname "America's Wartime Sweethearts." Their hit songs included "Boogie Woogie Bugle Boy" and "Don't Sit Under the Apple Tree." Over time, the Andrews Sisters sold more than 90 million records and recorded hundreds of songs!

The Andrew Sisters

U.S. SPORTS

World War II severely disrupted American sports. Numerous athletes, coaches, and other team staff members joined the military, leaving playing fields empty. The All-American Girls Professional Baseball League started in 1943 to fill empty ballparks after men were drafted into military service. More than 600 women between the ages of 16 and 27 played in the league for 12 seasons.

After the war ended, sports roared back to life. People were ready to cheer on their favorite teams and sports heroes. Most importantly, racial barriers were finally broken in the late 1940s, paving the way for athletes of color to play professional sports.

MVP

NAME:
TED WILLIAMS

SPORT:
Baseball

YEARS PLAYED:
1939 to 1960

TEAM:
Boston Red Sox

KNOWN FOR:
Regarded as one of the greatest hitters in baseball history, Williams is often referred to as the last player to hit over .400 in a single season.

JACKIE ROBINSON

Jackie Robinson made history in 1947 by becoming the first Black American baseball player to play in Major League Baseball (MLB). He started at first base for the Brooklyn Dodgers. Robinson's athleticism and courage helped him succeed in the face of discrimination and abuse. Today, Robinson is considered one of the greatest sports heroes of all time.

CITATION

Citation, a three-year-old Thoroughbred, raced his way to a Triple Crown victory in 1948. He won the 1948 Horse of the Year award and eventually became the first horse to earn more than one million dollars in prize money. Today, Citation is considered one of America's mightiest racehorses!

NBA

The National Basketball Association (NBA) was founded in 1946 as the Basketball Association of America. It launched with 11 teams divided into the Eastern Division and the Western Division. Three teams from the Eastern Division are still playing today. They are the Boston Celtics, the New York Knicks, and the Philadelphia Warriors, now known as the Golden State Warriors after they relocated in 1962.

BEN HOGAN

Ben Hogan was a professional golfer during the 1940s who dominated the sport, despite missing two seasons while he served in the military. Hogan was known for his precise ball-striking skills and intense focus. Over time, Hogan won 64 PGA Tours and 9 major championships. Today, Hogan is considered a golfing legend.

GLOBAL SPORTS

The outbreak of World War II also had a major impact on international sports. Many events were cancelled during the war years, including the 1940 and 1944 Olympic Games, the 1942 and 1946 FIFA World Cups, and the Tour de France. World War II also interrupted the tennis calendar. Wimbledon and the French Open tournaments were not played for six years.

After the war ended, people celebrated the return of international sporting events. Athletes around the world jumped back into their sports, their skills and sportsmanship undiminished by war. They would go on to wow fans in events that would captivate people around the world.

OLYMPICS OF THE 1940s

SUMMER 1948
LONDON, UNITED KINGDOM

WINTER 1948
ST. MORITZ, SWITZERLAND

Gretchen Fraser

1948 WINTER OLYMPICS

The Winter Olympics returned in 1948. These games, held in St. Moritz, Switzerland, were named the "Games of Renewal." Japan and Germany were not invited to participate. The Games featured 22 events and 669 athletes. Dick Button won the first gold medal for the U.S. for men's figure skating, and Gretchen Fraser won the first gold medal for an American skier.

1948 SUMMER OLYMPICS

The 1948 Summer Olympics were held in London, United Kingdom. Germany and Japan were not invited. The 1948 Summer Olympics became known as the "Austerity Olympics" due to Great Britain's economic struggles after the war ended. International athletes were housed in former army camps. Some nights, arenas were lit by car headlamps.

A FAST LEARNER!

American Bob Mathias, age 17, won the decathlon in the 1948 Summer Olympics four months after taking up the sport. He remains the youngest athlete to win a men's athletic event in Olympic history!

FANNY BLANKERS-KOEN

Fanny Blankers-Koen was a Dutch track and field athlete. While competing at the 1948 Summer Olympics in London, Blankers-Koen became the first woman to win four gold medals in a single games. She competed as a 30-year-old mother of two, earning her the nickname the "Flying Housewife." She returned to the Netherlands a national hero!

WIMBLEDON CHAMPIONSHIPS

Tennis players were ready to resume play for the Wimbledon Championships in 1946 after a six-year pause despite bomb damage to Centre Court's roof. Yvon Petra of France won the men's singles title, while Pauline Betz of the U.S. won the women's singles title.

TIMELINE

APRIL 9, 1940
Germany invades Denmark and Norway

SEPTEMBER 16, 1940
President Roosevelt signs the Selective Training and Service Act into law

NOVEMBER 5, 1940
President Roosevelt wins a third term in office

OCTOBER 23, 1941
Walt Disney releases *Dumbo,* the studio's fourth animated film

DECEMBER 7, 1941
Japanese planes bomb Pearl Harbor

DECEMBER 8, 1941
The U.S. enters World War II

FEBRUARY 19, 1942
President Roosevelt orders the internment of more than 120,000 Japanese Americans

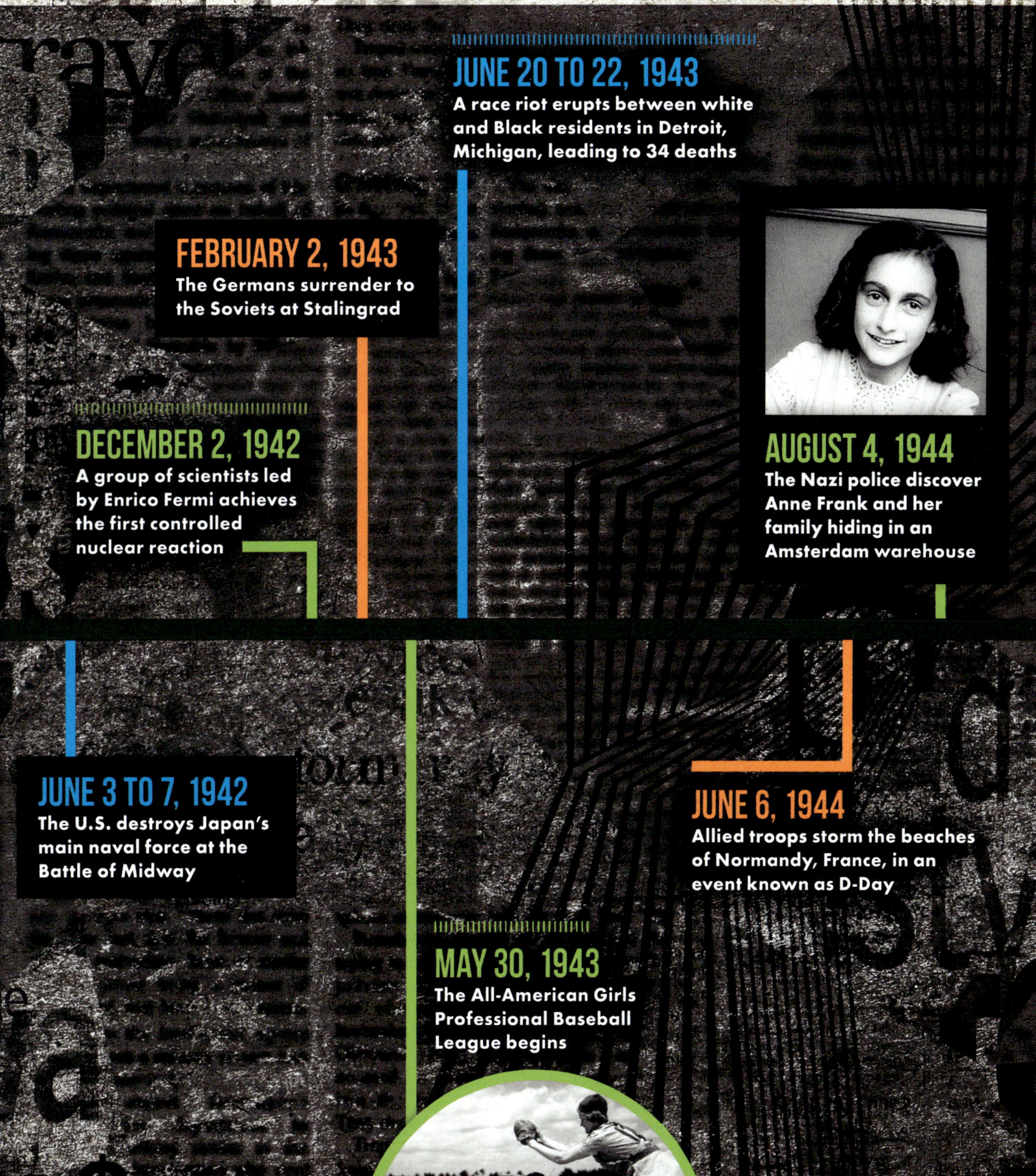

JUNE 20 TO 22, 1943
A race riot erupts between white and Black residents in Detroit, Michigan, leading to 34 deaths

FEBRUARY 2, 1943
The Germans surrender to the Soviets at Stalingrad

DECEMBER 2, 1942
A group of scientists led by Enrico Fermi achieves the first controlled nuclear reaction

AUGUST 4, 1944
The Nazi police discover Anne Frank and her family hiding in an Amsterdam warehouse

JUNE 3 TO 7, 1942
The U.S. destroys Japan's main naval force at the Battle of Midway

JUNE 6, 1944
Allied troops storm the beaches of Normandy, France, in an event known as D-Day

MAY 30, 1943
The All-American Girls Professional Baseball League begins

APRIL 12, 1945
President Roosevelt dies and is succeeded by Vice President Harry S. Truman

FEBRUARY 14, 1946
Professors at the University of Pennsylvania introduce ENIAC, the first modern computer

AUGUST 6 AND 9, 1945
The U.S. drops atomic bombs on the Japanese cities of Hiroshima and Nagasaki

APRIL 15, 1947
Jackie Robinson becomes the first Black American to play modern Major League Baseball

MAY 7, 1945
Germany surrenders to the Allies, ending World War II in Europe

JANUARY 10, 1946
The first session of the UN General Assembly opens in London

JULY 5, 1946
The bikini debuts in Paris, France

AUGUST 14 TO 15, 1947
Great Britain partitions India into India and Pakistan

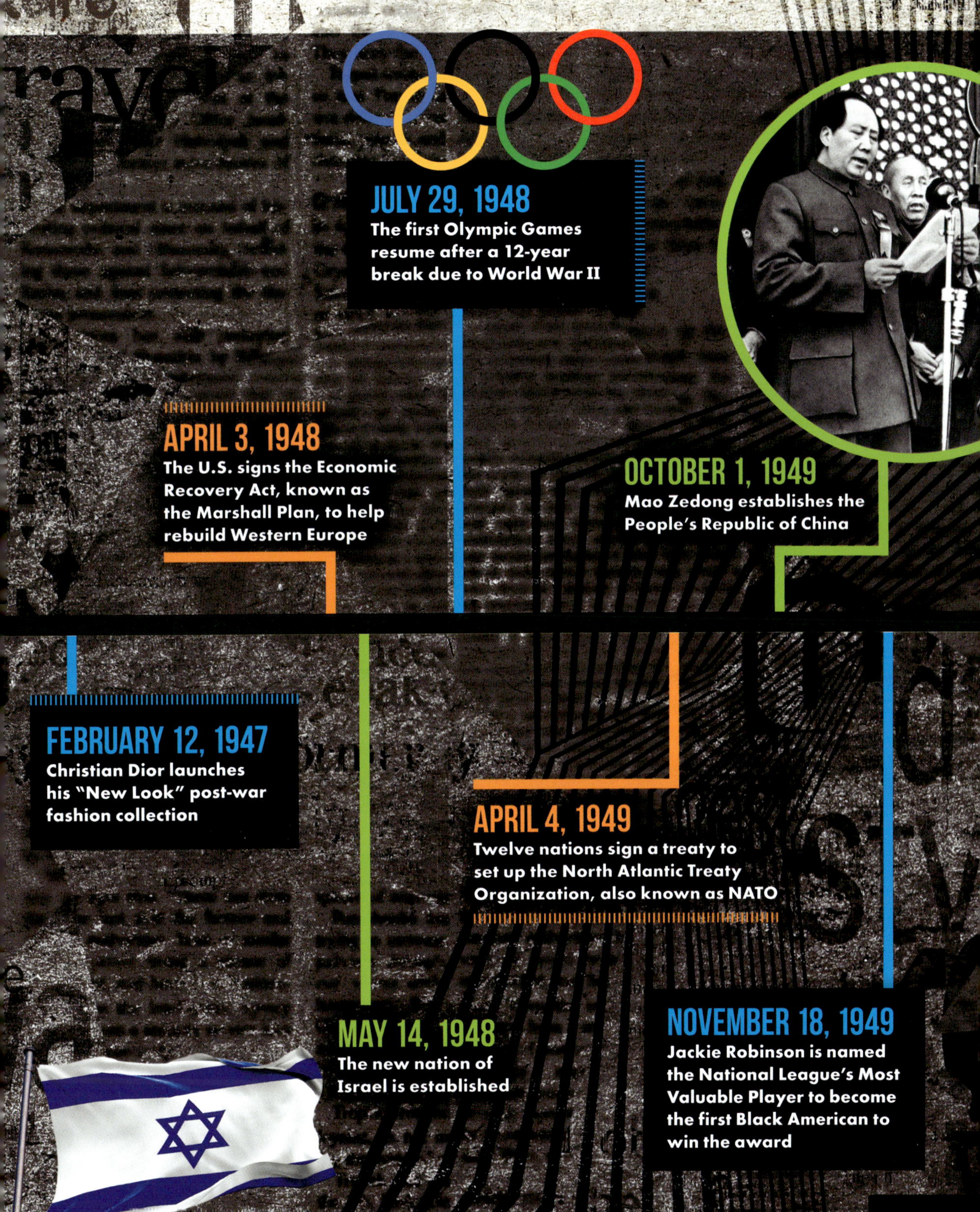

JULY 29, 1948
The first Olympic Games resume after a 12-year break due to World War II

APRIL 3, 1948
The U.S. signs the Economic Recovery Act, known as the Marshall Plan, to help rebuild Western Europe

OCTOBER 1, 1949
Mao Zedong establishes the People's Republic of China

FEBRUARY 12, 1947
Christian Dior launches his "New Look" post-war fashion collection

APRIL 4, 1949
Twelve nations sign a treaty to set up the North Atlantic Treaty Organization, also known as NATO

MAY 14, 1948
The new nation of Israel is established

NOVEMBER 18, 1949
Jackie Robinson is named the National League's Most Valuable Player to become the first Black American to win the award

GLOSSARY

allegory—a story that uses characters, objects, or other symbols to represent other ideas

antibiotic—a medicine that prevents small, harmful organisms from growing

atomic bombs—devices that release nuclear energy to cause destruction

Cold War—a conflict between the U.S. and the Soviet Union in the second half of the 1900s that did not break out into fighting

communism—a social system in which property and goods are controlled by the government

consumerism—the practice of buying and consuming goods and services, and the belief that doing so is good for the economy

discrimination—the act of treating someone unfairly because of race, gender, age, or other differences

draft—a system for selecting individuals from a group without their consent for military service

egalitarian—believing that everyone is equal and should have the same rights and opportunities

encrypted—related to hidden information that can be turned into secret code

film noir—dark, mysterious movies that often focus on crime in cities

Great Depression—a time in world history when many countries experienced economic crisis; the Great Depression began in 1929 and lasted through the 1930s.

internment camps—prison camps that people may be forced into during times of war; people in internment camps are not convicted of crimes.

isolationism—a policy where a country chooses to focus on itself and avoid getting involved with other countries

Jim Crow laws—U.S. laws that enforced racial segregation from the late 1870s until the 1960s

meteorologists—scientists who study the weather and atmosphere to predict and understand the weather

nuclear—used in or produced by a nuclear reaction; a nuclear reaction is a process in which the nucleus of an atom is split to create energy.

persecution—cruel and unfair treatment, especially toward those who differ in religion, race, or beliefs

racism—the belief that race is a fundamental part of human traits and that certain races are superior to others

ration—to use a limited amount of something, such as food or supplies

refugees—people who flee their home for safety

rhetoric—using words in a skillful way to influence people

satire—a form of art or writing that uses humor and exaggeration to reveal social, cultural, or personal flaws

segregation—the act of separating people based on their race

Soviet Union—short for the Union of Soviet Socialist Republics; the Soviet Union is a former country in Eastern Europe and western Asia made up of 15 republics or states that broke up in 1991.

succeeded—took over as president when the current president was unable to continue in office

synthetic—something that is made by people using chemicals

transfusions—medical procedures where donated blood is transferred into the bloodstreams of other people through narrow tubes placed in veins

transistor—a small device that can switch electric currents on or off or amplify them

Victory garden—a vegetable garden that a family or small community grew during World War II to supplement food rations

WRITE ABOUT IT!

- What do you think were the most important moments during the 1940s? Do you think these events affect life today? **Why?**

- If you saw someone being treated unfairly, what would you do and **why?**

- Which part of the 1940s would you have liked to experience? **Why?**

ALSO CHECK OUT

THE 1960S
THROUGH THE DECADES

THE 2000S
THROUGH THE DECADES

THE 1920S
THROUGH THE DECADES

INDEX

The images in this book are reproduced through the courtesy of: Pictorial Press Ltd/ Alamy Stock Photo, front cover (Frank), p. 43 (Frank); Sigma/ Wikipedia, front cover (medal); American portraiture/ Alamy Stock Photo, front cover (Robinson), pp. 38, 44 (Robinson); Florida Memory/ Wikipedia, front cover (girls); Felix Choo/ Alamy Stock Photo, front cover (book); sjvinyl/ Alamy Stock Photo, front cover (Fantasia); navy photo/ Wikipedia, front cover (explosion), p. 6 (explosion); Shawshots/ Alamy Stock Photo, pp. 3 (ration), 8 (ration) Rawpixel.com, pp. 3 (Rosie), 18-19 (Rosie); Bettmann/ Getty Images, pp. 3 (Olympics), 9 (G.I. Bill), 10-11, 15 (Zedong), 20, 23 (production), 34 (Fibber McGee), 37 (swing), 39 (Hogan), 40 (summer), 41 (all), 42 (1940); Gottlieb, William P./ Wikipedia, pp. 3 (Gillespie), 37 (Gillespie); US Government/ Wikipedia, p. 4 (stamp); LMPC/ Getty Images, pp. 4 (Bambi), 35 (Captain Midnight, Jack Armstrong); RGR Collection/ Alamy Stock Photo, p. 4 (Mickey); Glasshouse Images/ Alamy Stock Photo, p. 5 (all); Winai Tepsuttinun, p. 7 (gas); Photo Builder, p. 7 (newspaper); Artiom Photo, p. 7 (milk); phive2015, p. 7 (bread); AlenKadr, p. 7 (Coke); Chronicle/ Alamy Stock Photo, pp. 8 (women), 23 (penicillin); Irving Haberman/ IH Images/ Getty Images, p. 8 (suburb); Hulton Archive/ Getty Images, pp. 9 (internment), 35 (Texaco); FPG/ Getty Images, p. 9 (draft); Christian Mueller, p. 13 (memorial); GrummelJS/ Wikipedia, p. 13 (navy cross); Emerson Emory Papers/ Wikipedia, p. 13 (Miller); Joe Rosenthal/ Wikipedia, p. 14 (Iwo Jima); Underwood Archives/ Getty Images, pp. 14 (signing), 44 (1945); Keystone Features/ Getty Images, p. 14 (destruction); Charles Levy/ Wikipedia, p. 15 (bombings); Pictures from History/ Getty Images, p. 15 (Israel); enesdigital, p. 17 (Auschwitz); Air-in, p. 17 (memorial); PhotoQuest/ Getty Images, pp. 19 (women in service, segregation), 43 (baseball); GEC/ Wikipedia, p. 19 (women working); Windell Oskay/ Wikipedia, p. 21 (transistor); Purple Moon, p. 21 (tape); Historical/ Getty Images, p. 21 (ENIAC); Photo 12/ Alamy Stock Photo, p. 22 (children); Popperfoto/ Getty Images, pp. 22 (surgeons), 26 (seam line); Horace Abrahams/ Getty Images, p. 22 (donating); Harold M. Lambert/ Getty Images, pp. 24 (game), 29 (bubbles); Russell Lee/ Getty Images, p. 24 (segregation); Robert Landau/ Alamy Stock Photo, p. 24 (McDonalds); John Kisch Archive/ Getty Images, pp. 26-27; H. Armstrong Roberts/ ClassicStock/ Getty Images, p. 27 (Victory rolls); Lipnitzki/ Getty Images, p. 27 ("New Look"); Heritage Images/ Getty Images, p. 27 (suits); conzorb, p. 27 (bikini); Andrew Paterson/ Alamy Stock Photo, p. 28 (Scrabble); Patti McConville/ Stockimo/ Alamy Stock Photo, p. 28 (Slinky); Jeff Gilbert/ Alamy Stock Photo, p. 28 (Subbuteo); Karen Schueler, p. 29 (book); Camerique Archive/ Getty Images, p. 29 (trains); ClassicStock/ Alamy Stock Photo, p. 29 (dolls); Andrew Burton/ Getty Images, p. 30; Harper & Brothers/ Wikipedia, p. 31 (Native Son); Spencer Platt/ Getty Images, p. 31 (Curious George); RorySmith/ Wikipedia, p. 31 (Animal Farm); Cassowary Colorizations/ Wikipedia, p. 31 (Orwell); United Archives GmbH/ Alamy Stock Photo, p. 32 (Bugs Bunny); Allstar Picture Library Limited./ Alamy Stock Photo, p. 32 (Pinocchio); United Artists/ Wikipedia, p. 33 (Dictator); Allstar Picture Library Ltd/ Alamy Stock Photo, p. 33 (Fantasia); Sunset Boulevard/ Getty Images, p. 33 (Casablanca); rj lerich, p. 34 (radio); Michael Ochs Archives/ Getty Images, p. 36; MCA/ Wikipedia, p. 37 (sisters); HW/ FL/ RC/ WK/ Wikipedia, p. 39 (Robinson); ZenyattCi/ Wikipedia, p. 39 (Citation); Chris Ware/ Getty Images, p. 40 (winter); Collection Christophel/ Alamy Stock Photo, p. 42 (Dumbo); amzad, p. 44 (bikini); Mini Onion, p. 45 (flag); Pierre de Coubertin/ Wikipedia, p. 45 (Olympics); Mondadori Portfolio/ Getty Images, p. 45 (Zedong).